A CULTURE OF RESPECT

By

Jawanza Kunjufu

Illustrations by Harold Carr

Copyright 2007 by Jawanza Kunjufu

First edition, first printing

ISBN: 978-1-934155-06-6

Chicago, Illinois

What is respect?

To honor.

To be nice to people.

To be polite to people.

To be kind to people.

We must respect all adults.

We must respect all children.

Bad things happen when we do not respect teachers.

Bad things happen, when we do not respect each other.

Bad things happen when we do not respect each other.

Bad things happen when we do not respect ourselves.

How do we respect adults?

Good morning Mr. Jones (Principal).
Good morning students.

**How do we respect
adults?**

Good morning Mrs. Smith (Teacher)
Good morning students.

How do we respect adults?

Excuse me Mrs. Smith, may I ask Denise for a pencil?

How do we respect adults?

Take your cap off Darryl.
Yes sir Mr. Robinson.

How do we respect adults?

Thank you Mrs. Jackson.

How do we respect our classmates?

I'm sorry, I did not mean to bump into you.

How do we respect our classmates?

Would you please pass me the ketchup?

**How do we respect
each other?**

We never curse.
We never holler.
We are never rude.
We are always polite.

How do we respect each other?

We never use the "N" word.
We never use the "B" word.

What happens in a school of respect?

They have pizza parties.

What happens in a school of respect?

They go on field trips.

What happens in a school of respect?

They graduate.

What happens in a school of respect?

They go to college.

What happens in a school of respect?

They become great in their careers and their businesses.

WORDS OF RESPECT:	AFRICAN VALUES:
Good morning	Unity
Excuse me	Self-determination
Yes sir	Responsibility
No sir	Sharing
	Purpose
Yes ma'am	Creativity
No ma'am	Faith
	Truth
Thank you	Justice
You're welcome	Order
I'm sorry	Harmony
Please	Balance